بِسْمِ اللَّهِ الرَّحْمَٰنِ الرَّحِيمِ

In the name of Allah (swt), the Kind, the Merciful.

In honor of my late Jido Ali Ahmad Karnib, please recite Al Fatiha.

Created by Sabilla Karnib

Illustrated by Mahdi Tabatabaie Yazdi

Wisdom Writers 2 ~ Cursive Edition

First edition, 2025

 a_touch.of_faith

 atouchoffaith.com.au

 atouchoffaith313@gmail.com

Follow our instagram to support and stay up to date with new releases, behind the scenes content and much more!

Thank you for your kind support in helping bring 'Wisdom Writers' to the community and beyond.

Note for Teachers and Parents

In the name of God, the Kind, the Merciful.
Asalamu Alaykum,

A touch of faith is a small business focused on implementing a touch of faith in the everyday lives of families through words, creativity and a love for the Ahlul Bayt.

This handwriting book includes colouring, drawing, poetry, activities, Quran verses, hadiths, quotes, sentences and passages from Islamic literature that aim to develop and nurture:

- A child's love for God
- A child's love for the Ahlul Bayt
- Good character morals and ethics
- Positive affirmations
- Gratitude
- Creativity
- Reflection
- And Faith

Through implementing a touch of faith in a child's everyday life we aim to plant the seed of unconditional love and unwavering faith, towards our creator the Most Merciful.

This handwriting book contains 75 lessons and is targeted towards children ages 8 - 11.

Perfect for children learning and familiarising themselves with the cursive font. Part A introduces children to writing cursive letters and words. While part B familiarises children with this skill through sentences and passages in order to cement correct cursive letter formation. The text size starts out large and gets smaller as the lessons progress.

Every fifth lesson is focused on a member of the Ahlul Bayt, and every sixth lesson is based on a verse from the Holy Quran.

Each lesson in this handwriting book provides an opportunity for the child to draw or colour, in order to improve drawing skills, enhance their creativity and have fun!

We hope you enjoy every lesson and appreciate your support in bringing 'Wisdom Writers' to the community and beyond!

God Bless,
A Touch of Faith

Abbreviations:
(pbuh) - May peace be upon him.
(as) - *Alayhis Salaam* - May peace be upon him.
(sa) - *Salaamullah Alayha* - May peace be upon her.
(ajtfs) - *Ajjallahu ta'aala fashajahush shareef* - May God hasten his reappearance.

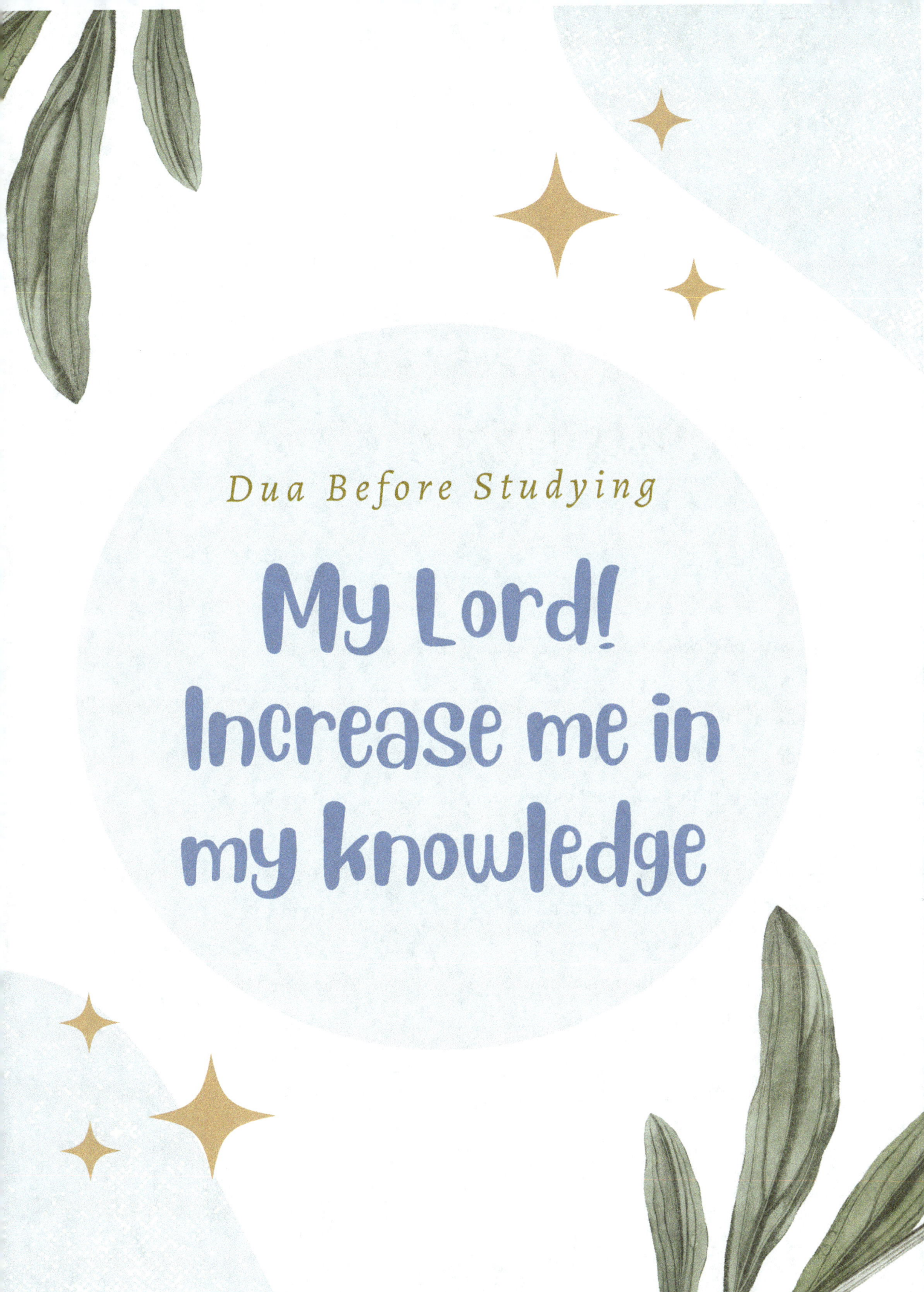

Ahlul Bayt Lessons Contents Page

Lesson 5 - The 12 Imams .... Page 11

Lesson 10 - Prophet Muhammad (pbuh)..................... Page 21

Lesson 15 - Lady Fatima (sa) .... Page 31

Lesson 20 - Imam Ali (as) .... Page 41

Lesson 25 - Imam Hasan (as).. Page 53

Lesson 30 - Imam Husain (as) .... Page 63

Lesson 35 - Imam Ali Zain al Abideen (as) .... Page 73

Lesson 40 - Imam Muhammad al Baqir (as) .... Page 83

Lesson 45 - Imam Jafar as Sadiq (as) .... Page 93

Lesson 50 - Imam Musa al Kadhim (as) .... Page 103

Lesson 55 - Imam Ali ar Rida (as) .... Page 113

Lesson 60 - Imam Muhammad at Taqi (as) .... Page 123

Lesson 65 - Imam Ali al Hadi (as) .... Page 133

Lesson 70 - Imam Hasan al Askari (as) .... Page 143

Lesson 75 - Imam Mahdi (ajtfs) .... Page 153

Quran Lessons Contents Page

Lesson 6 - Quran .... Page 13

Lesson 12 - Quran .... Page 25

Lesson 18 - Quran .... Page 37

Lesson 24 - Quran .... Page 51

Lesson 29 - Quran .... Page 61

Lesson 36 - Quran .... Page 75

Lesson 42 - Quran .... Page 87

Lesson 48 - Quran .... Page 99

Lesson 54 - Quran .... Page 111

Lesson 59 - Quran .... Page 121

Lesson 66 - Quran .... Page 135

Part A

INTRODUCTION INTO CURSIVE

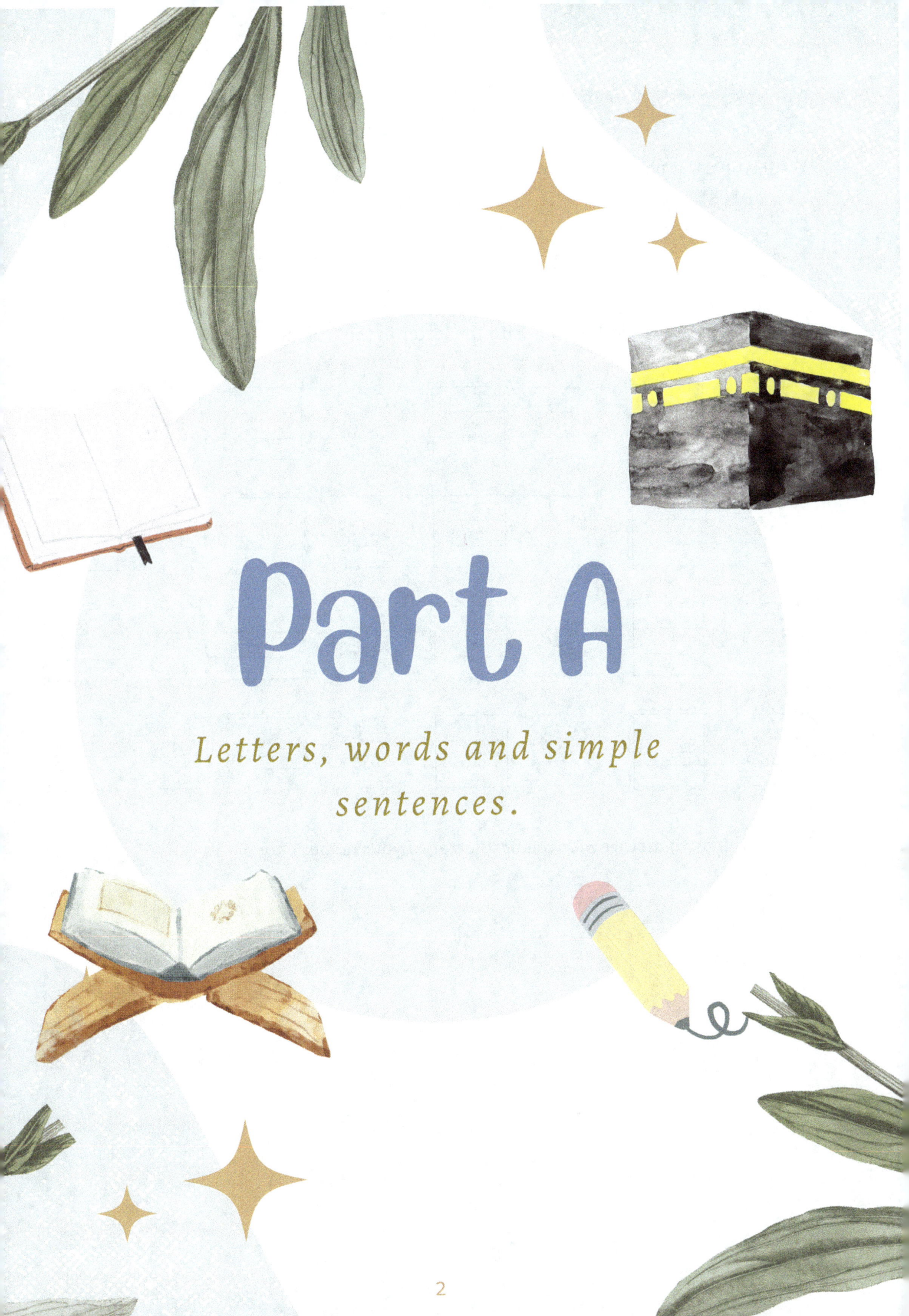

Part A

Letters, words and simple sentences.

LESSON 1 – LETTERS

Write your first name on the line below.

Carefully trace each letter and write the letter in the frame.

Aa Bb Cc Dd
Ee Ff Gg Hh
Ii Jj Kk Ll
Mm Nn Oo Pp

Draw 5 things that start with the first letter of your name.

LESSON 1 - LETTERS

Write your last name on the line below.

Carefully trace each letter and write the letter in the frame.

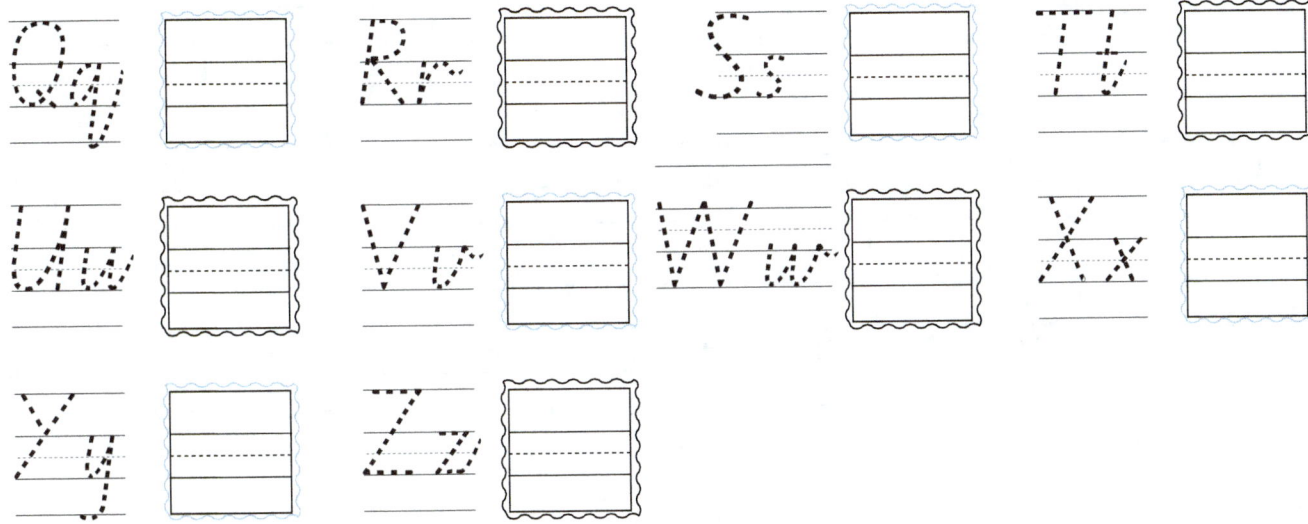

Colour the picture.

LESSON 2 - LETTER A + B

Trace and write the letter on the line.

Trace and copy the word.

Draw something amazing.

LESSON 2 - LETTER A + B

Trace and write the letter on the line.

Trace the words.

bright
bright

beautiful
beautiful

blessed
blessed

Draw something bright and beautiful that you have been blessed with.

6

LESSON 3 - LETTER C + D

Trace and write the letter on the line.

Trace the words.

calm

calm

caring

caring

creative

creative

Colour the picture.

LESSON 3 - LETTER C + D

Trace and write the letter on the line.

D | D D D D
D | D D D D
d | d d d d
d | d d d d

Trace and copy the sentence.

Dare to dream.

Draw a hope or wish for your future self.

LESSON 4 – LETTER E + F

Trace and write the letter on the line.

Trace and copy the word.

Earth

Draw planet Earth.

LESSON 4 - LETTER E + F

Trace and write the letter on the line.

Trace the words.

free
free
friendly
friendly
faithful
faithful

Colour the picture.

LESSON 5 - THE 12 IMAMS

Trace the names of the first six Imams.

Imam Ali (as)

Imam Hasan (as)

Imam Husain (as)

Imam Ali Zain al Abideen (as)

Imam Muhammad al Baqir (as)

Imam Jafar as Sadiq (as)

Colour the picture.

LESSON 5 - THE 12 IMAMS

Trace the names of the last six Imams.

Imam Musa al Kadhim (as)

Imam Ali ar Rida (as)

Imam Muhammad al Taqi (as)

Imam Ali al Hadi (as)

Imam Hasan al Askari (as)

Imam Muhammad al Mahdi (ajtfs)

Copy the sentence.

We have twelve Imams.

LESSON 6 – QURAN

وَأَحْسِن كَمَآ أَحْسَنَ ٱللَّهُ إِلَيْكَ

And do good to others as Allah has done good to you

Quran 28:77

LESSON 6 - QURAN

Trace the hadith from Imam Ali (as) in any colour.

The doer of good is better than the good itself.

- Imam Ali (as)

Trace and copy the sentences.

Think good thoughts.

Do good deeds.

Trace the sentence from 'Dua Arafa' by Imam Husain (as).

Please decree for us that which is good and make us the people of goodness.

Nahjul Balagha 'Peak of Eloquence' - Imam Ali (as)
Dua Arafah - Imam Husain (as)

LESSON 7 - LETTER G + H

Trace and write the letter on the line.

Trace the words.

gentle
gentle
gifted
gifted
grateful
grateful

Colour the picture.

LESSON 7 - LETTER G + H

Trace and write the letter on the line.

Trace the words.

happy
happy
humble
humble
hopeful
hopeful

Colour the picture.

LESSON 8 - LETTER I + J

Trace and write the letter on the line.

Trace and copy the words.

intelligent
intelligent

imagination
imagination

Colour the picture.

LESSON 8 - LETTER I + J

Trace and write the letter on the line.

Trace and copy the words.

jolly
jolly

joyful
joyful

Draw something that makes you smile whenever you think about it.

LESSON 9 – LETTER K + L

Trace and write the letter on the line.

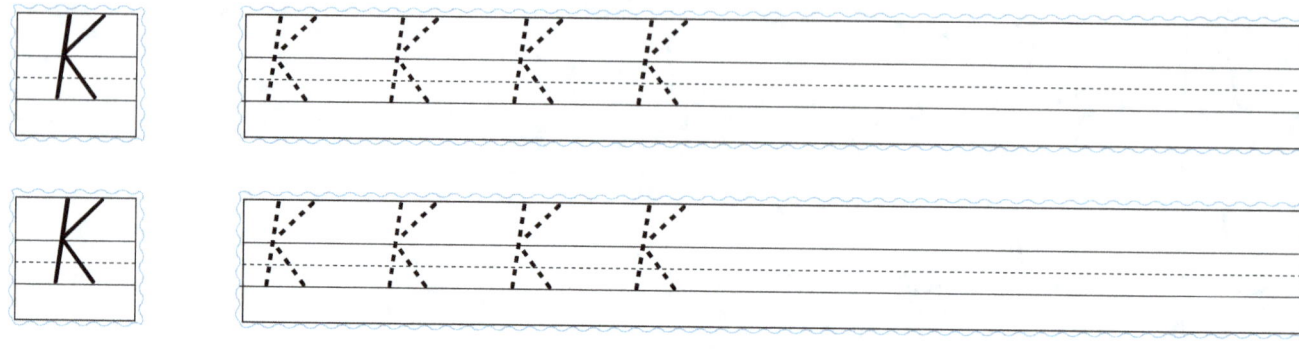

Trace and copy the word.

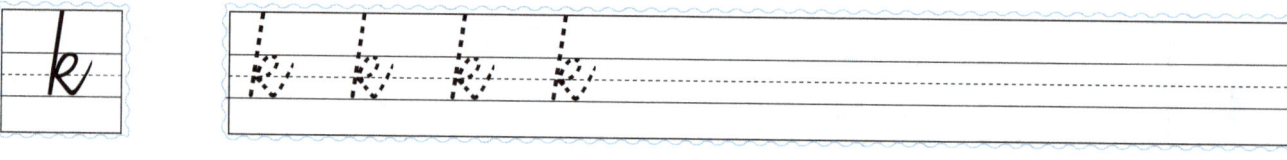

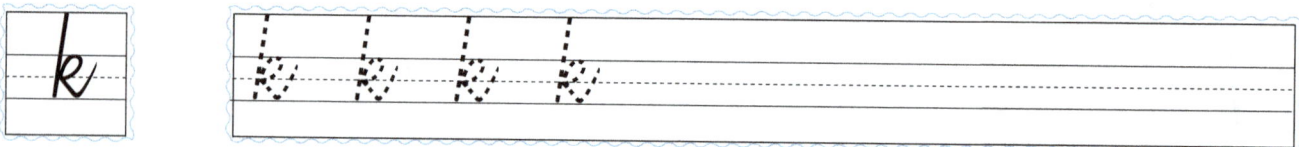

What act of kindness did you do today? Draw it in the box below.

LESSON 9 - LETTER K + L

Trace and write the letter on the line.

Trace the words.

live
live
love
love
laugh
laugh

Colour the picture.

LESSON 10 - PROPHET MUHAMMAD (PBUH)

Copy the sentence.

Prophet Muhammad (pbuh) is the last Prophet.

Trace the poem.

God is always by my side, with the Quran, Ahlul Bayt and Prophet Muhammad (pbuh) as my beloved guide.

Colour the picture.

LESSON 10 - PROPHET MUHAMMAD (PBUH)

Copy the sentence.

Prophet Muhammad (pbuh) was truthful and trustworthy.

Trace the sentences.

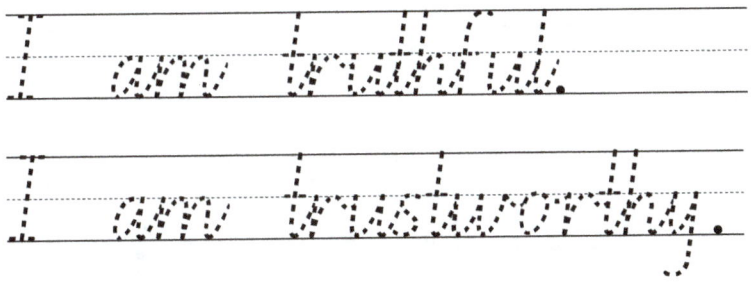

I am truthful.
I am trustworthy.

Fun Fact:
Prophet Muhammad (pbuh) was born in the year of the Elephant.

Colour the Mosque of Prophet Muhammad (pbuh).

Fun Fact:
God sent down 124,000 Prophets. The first Prophet was Prophet Adam (pbuh) and the last Prophet was Prophet Muhammad (pbuh).

Fun Fact:
The Mosque of Prophet Muhammad (pbuh) is located in Madina.

LESSON 11 - LETTER M + N

Trace and write the letter on the line.

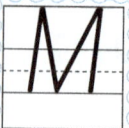 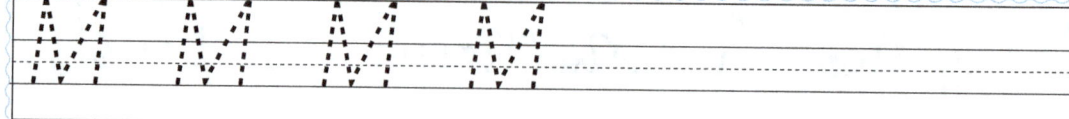

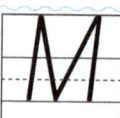 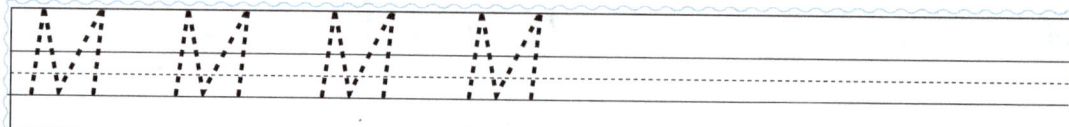

 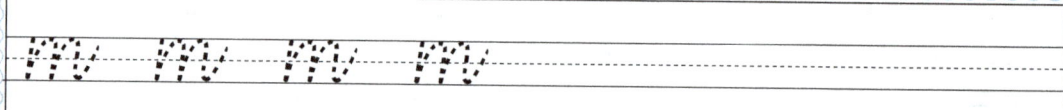

Trace and copy the word.

Colour the picture.

23

LESSON 11 - LETTER M + N

Trace and write the letter on the line.

Trace the words.

neat

neat

nice

nice

nature

nature

Look out your window and draw what you see.

LESSON 12 - QURAN

$$\text{وَهُوَ مَعَكُمْ أَيْنَ مَا كُنْتُمْ}$$

And He is with you wherever you are

Quran 57:4

LESSON 12 - QURAN

Trace the sentence.

One day you'll look back and see that God was with you every step of the way.

Copy the sentences.

Where there is God, there is hope. Since God is always with us, there is always hope.

Use colours and patterns to show how you are feeling today.

LESSON 13 - LETTER O + P

Trace and write the letter on the line.

O O O O O

O O O O O

o o o o o

o o o o o

Trace and copy the words.

outstanding

outstanding

overjoyed

overjoyed

Draw a moment when you felt truly proud of yourself.

LESSON 13 - LETTER O + P

Trace and write the letter on the line.

Trace the words.

polite

polite

patient

patient

prayer

prayer

Colour the picture.

LESSON 14 - LETTER Q + R

Trace and write the letter on the line.

Trace and copy the word.

Quran

Colour the picture.

LESSON 14 - LETTER Q + R

Trace and write the letter on the line.

Trace the words.

radiant

radiant

resilient

resilient

relaxed

relaxed

Draw something that makes you feel relaxed.

LESSON 15 - LADY FATIMA (SA)

Trace the passage.

Lady Fatima (sa) is the daughter of Prophet Muhammad (pbuh) and the wife of Imam Ali (as). Not a single picture of her face exists yet her name continues to inspire thousands around the world.

Colour the picture.

LESSON 15 - LADY FATIMA (SA)

Copy the sentence.

Lady Fatima (sa) is our role model and the leader of the women of Heaven.

Trace the sentences.

I am strong like Fatima (sa).
I am brave like Fatima (sa).
I am humble like Fatima (sa).
I am modest like Fatima (sa).
I am kind like Fatima (sa).
I am pure like Fatima (sa).

LESSON 16 - LETTER S + T

Trace and write the letter on the line.

 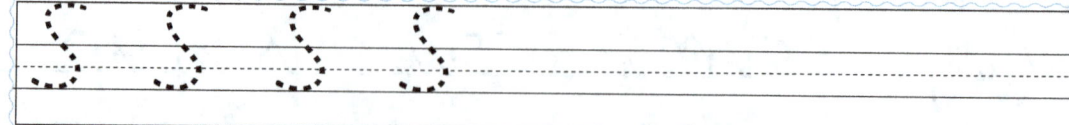

 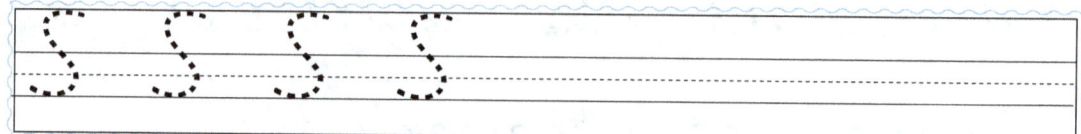

 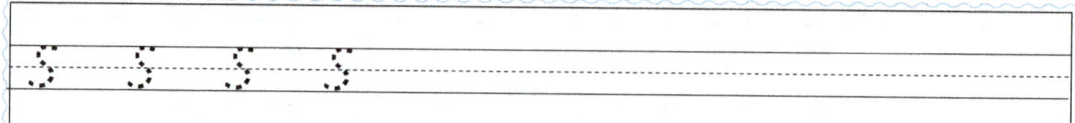

Trace the words.

safe

safe

smart

smart

strong

strong

Draw a place where you feel safe.

33

LESSON 16 - LETTER S + T

Trace and write the letter on the line.

T T T T

T T T T

t t t t

t t t t

Trace the words.

thankful

thankful

talented

talented

trustworthy

trustworthy

Draw something you are thankful for.

LESSON 17 - LETTER U + V

Trace and write the letter on the line.

Trace the words.

unique

unique

uplifting

uplifting

understanding

understanding

Draw a person who has inspired you.

LESSON 17 - LETTER U + V

Trace and write the letter on the line.

Trace the words.

valiant

valiant

vibrant

vibrant

virtuous

virtuous

DICTIONARY:

Valiant - Showing courage in both spirit and actions.

Vibrant - Full of life, energy and excitement.

Virtuous - Behaving in a very good and moral way.

LESSON 18 - QURAN

If you are grateful I will certainly give you more

Quran 14:7

LESSON 18 - QURAN

Trace the sentence.

Be grateful to God in every way, and you will find that God is generous in every way.

Copy the sentence.

Gratitude turns what we have into enough.

Draw something you are grateful for.

LESSON 19 - LETTER W + X

Trace and write the letter on the line.

W W W W W

W W W W W

w w w w w

w w w w w

Trace the words.

warm

warm

wise

wise

wonderful

wonderful

Colour the picture.

39

LESSON 19 - LETTER W + X

Trace and write the letter on the line.

Trace and copy the word.

excellent

excellent

excellent

excellent

Draw a portrait of someone near you.

LESSON 20 - IMAM ALI (AS)

Copy the sentence.

Imam Ali (as) is the first Imam.

Trace the sentence.

Imam Ali (as) was brave, compassionate and the only person to be born in the Kaaba.

-- ABOUT --
Name: Imam Ali (as)
Title: Commander of the Faithful
Imam Number: 1
Buried in: Najaf, Iraq

Colour the picture.

LESSON 20 - IMAM ALI (AS)

Trace the passage from the poem 'Ali, the superhero of humanity'.

Ali, the superhero of humanity,
Ali, the paragon of spirituality,
Ali, the great figure of history,
Ali, the superman of virtue,
Ali, the ideal man of human value,
Ali, the warrior of bravery,
Ali, the symbol of purity,
Ali, the model of generosity,
Ali, the support of the Prophet.

Dictionary :
Paragon ~ A model of excellence or perfection.

LESSON 21 - LETTER Y + Z

Trace and write the letter on the line.

Trace and copy the word.

youthful
youthful
youthful
youthful

Colour the picture.

LESSON 21 - LETTER Y + Z

Trace and write the letter on the line.

Draw a picture inspired by your culture.

LESSON 22 – PART A REVIEW

Using cursive, write your first name on the line below.

Carefully trace each letter and write the letter in the frame.

Aa   Bb   Cc   Dd

Ee   Ff   Gg   Hh

Ii   Jj   Kk   Ll

Mm   Nn   Oo   Pp

Colour the picture.

LESSON 22 - PART A REVIEW

Using cursive, write your last name on the line below.

Carefully trace each letter and write the letter in the frame.

Qq   Rr   Ss   Tt

Uu   Vv   Ww   Xx

Yy   Zz

Draw 5 things that start with the first letter of your last name.

Part B

SENTENCES AND PASSAGES

Part B

Tracing and writing sentences, passages, poems and hadith.

LESSON 23

Look, trace and copy the sentence.

I love God and God loves me.

Trace and copy the words.

loved

safe

kind

Colour the picture.

LESSON 23

Trace the passage.

God made everything. He made the blue sky, the green grass, the tall trees and the beautiful ocean.

Draw the scene described in the passage above.

LESSON 24 - QURAN

وَرَحْمَتِي وَسِعَتْ كُلَّ شَيْءٍ

My mercy encompasses everything

Quran 7:156

LESSON 24 - QURAN

Trace the sentence.

God is the Most Merciful, His mercy is infinite and we would never be able to count all of God's blessings.

Copy the sentence.

Don't let one worry make you forget a thousand blessings.

Draw something God has blessed you with.

LESSON 25 - IMAM HASAN (AS)

Copy the sentence.

Imam Hasan (as) is the second Imam. He was pious and pure.

-- ABOUT --
Name: Imam Hasan (as)
Title: The Chosen One
Imam Number: 2
Buried in: Jannat al-Baqi cemetery, Madina

Trace the hadith from Imam Hasan (as) in any colour.

Treat others similar to the way you would like for them to treat you.

- Imam Hasan (as)

Bihar-ul-Anwar, vol. 78, p. 116

LESSON 25 - IMAM HASAN (AS)

Trace the passage.

Imam Hasan (as) was the first son of Imam Ali (as) and Lady Fatima (sa). He was the first grandson of Prophet Muhammad (pbuh) and when he was born Prophet Muhammad (pbuh) named him Hasan and recited the adhan in his right ear and the iqamah in his left ear.

Colour the picture.

LESSON 26

Look, trace and copy the sentence.

Do small things with great love.

Do small things with great love.

Do small things with great love.

Colour the picture.

LESSON 26

Copy the sentences.

Look back and thank God.

Look forward and trust God.

Colour the picture.

LESSON 27

Trace the sentences.

I am grateful for my parents.
I am grateful for my family.
I am grateful for my home.

Copy the sentence.

God has given me so many blessings.

Trace and copy the words.

grateful

thankful

blessed

Colour the picture.

LESSON 27

Trace and copy the sentence.

Start your day with Bismillah.

Trace and copy the sentences.

Find beauty in the small things.

Gratitude turns what we have into enough.

Draw someone you love and are grateful for.

LESSON 28

Trace the sentence.

Everyday is a new day to become a better person.

Look, trace and copy the sentence.

Be the reason someone smiles.

Be the reason someone smiles.

Colour the picture.

LESSON 28

Copy the sentence.

Helping one person might not change the whole world, but it can change the world for one person.

What act of kindness did you do today? Draw it in the box below.

LESSON 29 - QURAN

أَلَا بِذِكْرِ ٱللَّهِ تَطْمَئِنُّ ٱلْقُلُوبُ

Surely in the remembrance of Allah do hearts find comfort

Quran 13:28

LESSON 29 - QURAN

Trace the sentences.

Through God's love, the heart gains strength. O Allah attach our hearts to you.

Trace the passage from the poem 'Remember just remember'.

When things are down and you are are out of your mind; Remember just remember Allah is the kind. When no one wants to listen or is willing to lend an ear; Remember just remember Allah is always ready to hear. When you're all done and your pain has no end; Remember just remember Allah is your friend.

An Anthology of Islamic Poetry:
('Remember just remember')

LESSON 30 - IMAM HUSAIN (AS)

Copy the sentences.

Imam Husain (as) is the third Imam. He was courageous and stood up against oppression and injustice.

Dictionary :
Oppression ~ When a person or group of people who have power use it in a way that is not fair, unjust or cruel.

Trace the hadith from Imam Husain (as) in any colour.

Wisdom will not be complete except by following the truth.
- Imam Husain (as)

Biharol Anwar, Vol. 78, P. 127

LESSON 30 - IMAM HUSAIN (AS)

Trace the sentence.

I am brave, courageous, patient and forgiving like Imam Husain (as).

-- ABOUT --
Name: Imam Husain (as)
Title: The Master of Martyrs
Imam Number: 3
Buried in: Karbala, Iraq

Colour the picture.

Fun Fact:
Over 20 million people walk from Najaf to Karbala every year during Muharram to visit the shrine of Imam Husain (as). This walk is famously known as the Arbaeen.

LESSON 31

Copy the sentences.

God is always with me.

I can always find comfort in God.

I can talk to God about anything.

Colour the picture.

LESSON 31

Trace the passage from the poem 'A man so great'.

Ali, a name so great,
A man whose deeds we celebrate.
A symbol of courage,
A symbol of bravery.
A symbol of compassion,
A symbol of dignity,
But more importantly,
A symbol of knowledge,
To which the Prophet states;
"I am the city of knowledge and
Ali is its gates".

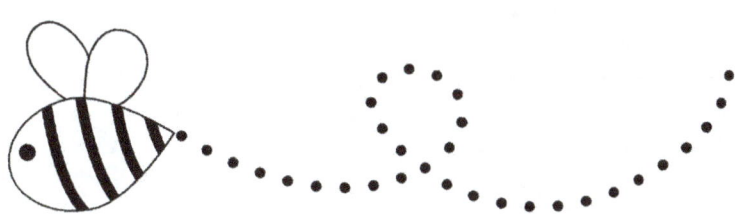

'A man so great' - Nabaa Alhameed

LESSON 32

Copy the sentences.

I believe in myself and what I can do.

The challenges I face make me stronger.

Trace and copy the sentences.

Work hard.

Dream big.

Never give up.

Draw your future self.

LESSON 32

Trace the prayer.

Dear God, please teach me to be patient and to have faith.

Copy the sentence.

Those who leave everything in God's hands will eventually see God's hands in everything.

Colour the picture.

MY WISH   GOD'S PLAN

LESSON 33

Trace the letter and sign your name on the dotted line.

Dear Allah,

I just wanted to say Alhamdulilah

and thank you for everything.

Lots of love, ...

Draw your local mosque in the box below.

LESSON 33

Trace and copy the sentence.

Flowers bloom in every heart that remembers Allah (swt).

Colour the picture.

LESSON 34

Trace the prayer.

O Allah, when I lose hope, help me remember that your love is greater than anything.

Copy the sentence.

Let your faith in Allah (swt) be bigger than your fear.

Colour the picture.

LESSON 34

Trace the hadith from Imam Ali (as) in any colour.

Place your hope in Allah.
– Imam Ali (as)

Trace the passage.

God knows exactly what you are going through. He is always there to listen, to comfort and to help you through your toughest times.

Draw a picture that represents hope.

Fun Fact:
The name Allah is written over 2500 times in the Quran.

Nahjul Balagha 'Peak of Eloquence' - Imam Ali (as)

LESSON 35 – IMAM ALI ZAIN AL ABIDEEN (AS)

Copy the sentence.

Imam Sajjad (as) is the fourth Imam.

Trace the passage.

As Sajjad means the worshipper of Allah (swt). Imam Ali Zain al Abideen (as) loved to pray, worship and talk to Allah (swt) all the time.

Colour the picture.

LESSON 35 - IMAM ALI ZAIN AL ABIDEEN (AS)

Trace the hadith from Imam Sajjad (as) in any colour.

The closest to God is the most well-mannered

- Imam Zain al Abideen (as)

Trace the poem.

How beautiful is sujood,

you whisper on the ground,

and you're heard in the highest of

the heavens.

-- ABOUT --
Name: Imam Zain al Abideen (as)
Title: Worshipper of Allah (swt)
Imam Number: 4
Buried in: Jannat al-Baqi cemetery, Madina

Tuhaf Al-Uqul

LESSON 36 - QURAN

وَتَوَكَّلْ عَلَى ٱللَّهِ ۚ وَكَفَىٰ بِٱللَّهِ وَكِيلًا

Put your trust in Allah, for Allah is sufficient as a Trustee of affairs

Quran 33:3

LESSON 36 - QURAN

Copy the sentence.

I am patient and trust God with all my heart.

Trace the sentences.

Allah (swt) can make the impossible, be possible. Be patient and trust His wisdom.

Trace and copy the words.

God

love

faith

trust

hope

Draw a candle in a dark room.

LESSON 37

Trace the sentence.

You are meant to shine from the inside out, you have a heart made of gold so don't let others dim your sparkling light.

Copy the sentence.

Your character is a reflection of your inner beauty.

Create a drawing using only two colours.

LESSON 37

Trace the sentences.

Speak in such a way that others love to listen to you. Listen in such a way that others love to speak to you.

Copy the sentence.

God is forgiving and I can forgive others too.

Colour the picture.

LESSON 38

Copy the sentence from the morning and evening dua of Imam Sajjad (as).

O God, bless Muhammad and his Household and give us success in this day of ours.

Copy the sentences.

I am thankful for today.

I am grateful for today.

I will make the most of today.

Create a drawing using only circles.

The Psalms of Islam 'Al-Sahifat Al-Sajjadiyya' -
Imam Zain al Abideen (as) : Supplication 6

LESSON 38

Trace the hadith from Imam Ali ar Rida (as) in any colour.

He who wishes to be the strongest of all should rely on Allah.

- Imam Ali ar Rida (as)

Trace and copy the sentence.

Your relationship with God is a precious gift.

Draw a picture that represents faith

Fiqh-Ur-Reza (A.S.). P 358

LESSON 39

Trace the passage.

Allah (swt) is the Creator of the universe and the light of the heavens and the Earth. He inspires flowers to bloom, mountains to rise and only He is worthy of being worshipped.

Colour the picture.

LESSON 39

Copy the passage on the previous page.

Draw a picture inspired by the passage on the previous page.

LESSON 40 - IMAM MUHAMMAD AL BAQIR (AS)

Copy the sentence.

Imam Baqir (as) is the fifth Imam.

Trace the sentence.

Imam Muhammad al Baqir (as) was known as al Baqir because of his tremendous knowledge.

-- ABOUT --
Name: Imam Muhammad al Baqir (as)
Title: The one who possesses great knowledge
Imam Number: 5
Buried in: Jannat al-Baqi cemetery, Madina

Colour the picture.

LESSON 40 - IMAM MUHAMMAD AL BAQIR (AS)

Trace the hadith from Imam Baqir (as) in any colour.

Seeking knowledge is worship

- Imam Baqir (as)

Trace the hadiths from Prophet Muhammad (pbuh).

Learning knowledge, putting it to practice and teaching it to others is a form of charity for man.

No combination is better than that of knowledge and patience.

Copy the hadith from Prophet Muhammad (pbuh).

Knowledge is a believers friend.

Ibn Hamadun, al-Tadhkira p.26
Nahj Al-Fasahah

LESSON 41

Trace the passage from the morning and evening dua of Imam Sajjad (as).

Praise belongs to God,

The First, without a first before Him,

The Last, without a last behind Him.

Copy passage from the poem 'His words'.

Allah's pleasure is our only aim,

Glorified be His name.

Colour the picture.

The Psalms of Islam 'Al-Sahifat Al-Sajjadiyya' - Imam Zain al Abideen (as) : Supplication 6

An Anthology of Islamic Poetry - (Excerpt of 'His Words')

LESSON 41

Copy the sentences.

God gives me strength.

God gives me peace.

God is always with me.

Colour the picture.

86

LESSON 42 - QURAN

وَقَضَىٰ رَبُّكَ أَلَّا تَعْبُدُوٓا۟ إِلَّآ إِيَّاهُ وَبِٱلْوَٰلِدَيْنِ إِحْسَٰنًا

And your Lord has decreed that you worship none but Him, and be good to your parents

Quran 17:23

LESSON 42 - QURAN

Trace the hadith from Prophet Muhammad (pbuh) in any colour.

The look of a child towards his parents out of love for them is an act of worship.

- Prophet Muhammad (pbuh)

Trace and copy the sentences.

Treat your parents with respect.

Treat your parents with kindness.

Treat your parents with care.

Biharul Anwar, Volume 74, Page 80

LESSON 43

Copy the hadith from Imam Ali (as).

If a person has a good idea about you, make his idea be true.

Trace the sentence.

Beautify your character so that you may spread goodness to those around you and walk the path that leads to God.

Draw a three-part comic strip showing a time you helped others this week.

Nahjul Balagha 'Peak of Eloquence' - Imam Ali (as)

LESSON 43

Trace the passage below.

Do random acts of kindness everyday without expecting anything in return and see how wonderful you feel and how amazing you make others feel. Be the reason someone believes in the goodness of other people.

Colour the picture.

LESSON 44

Copy the sentence.

Kindness can change the world.

Trace the hadith from Imam Ali ar Rida (as).

The true Muslim never teases others with his hand or tongue.

Trace and copy the sentences.

Be kind.

Be loving.

Be caring.

Colour the picture.

Aoyun Akhbar Ar Reza (as) - VOL 2, pg 24

LESSON 44

Trace the passage below.

Never underestimate the power of a hug, a smile, a kind word, a listening ear, an honest compliment, or the smallest act of caring, all of which have the potential to turn a life around.

Draw one of your favourite memories.

LESSON 45 - IMAM JAFAR AS SADIQ (AS)

Copy the sentence.

Imam Jafar (as) is the sixth Imam.

Trace the sentence.

Imam Jafar (as) was known as as Sadiq which means the truthful one.

Trace the hadith from Imam Jafar as Sadiq (as) in any colour.

Oh God, give me success in what You love and in what makes You content.

- Imam Jafar as Sadiq (as)

-- ABOUT --
Name: Imam Jafar as Sadiq (as)
Title: The Truthful One
Imam Number: 6
Buried in: Jannat al-Baqi cemetery, Madina

LESSON 45 - IMAM JAFAR AS SADIQ (AS)

Trace the passage below.

Imam Jafar as Sadiq (as) laid the foundation of an Islamic University in Madina to teach students in different fields of knowledge. Hundreds of students from all over the world came to Madina to join the classes of the Imam. Many of his students went on to become prominent scholars in various fields.

Colour the picture.

LESSON 46

Trace the passage below.

I am a beloved creation of Allah (swt). I am strong because He is with me. I am kind because Prophet Muhammad (pbuh) is my role model. I am grateful for the blessings Allah (swt) has given me. I am patient, knowing that His timing is perfect.

Colour the picture.

LESSON 46

Trace the passage below.

I am brave, for Allah (swt) is my protector. I am compassionate, showing mercy to all creatures. I am confident for Allah (swt) has a plan for me. I am generous, sharing with those in need. I am respectful towards my parents and elders and I am forgiving as Allah (swt) forgives me.

Colour the picture.

LESSON 47

Copy the sentence.

There is no greater power than faith.

Trace the sentence.

Always pray to have eyes that see the best in people, a heart that forgives, and a soul that never loses faith in God.

Colour the picture.

LESSON 47

Trace and copy the passage.

Courage isn't the absence of fear but doing the right thing regardless of it. Be strong because things will get better. It may be stormy now, but it never rains forever.

Colour the picture.

LESSON 48 - QURAN

يَـٰٓأَيُّهَا ٱلَّذِينَ ءَامَنُواْ ٱسْتَعِينُواْ بِٱلصَّبْرِ وَٱلصَّلَوٰةِ ۚ إِنَّ ٱللَّهَ مَعَ ٱلصَّـٰبِرِينَ

O believers! Seek comfort through patience and prayer. Allah is truly with those who are patient.

Quran 2:153

LESSON 48 - QURAN

Trace the passage from the poem 'Pillars of faith' in any colour.

Salat is a form of worship for you and me. We bow down our heads only to Allah, you see.

Trace and copy the sentences.

When it hurts, pray.

God hears me when I pray.

Copy the hadith from Imam Jafar as Sadiq (as).

A person who knows the value of patience cannot bear to be without it.

An Anthology of Islamic Poetry - ('Pillars of Faith' by souladvisor)
Lantern of the Path - Imam Jafar as Sadiq (as)

LESSON 49

Trace the passage from the poem 'The Islamic way'.

Each morning my ears hear the Adhan before prayer. With my hands I perform Wudhu and I do it with care. To the masjid I walk briskly upon both of my feet. Giving salams to all the Muslims I meet. While making sujood, I get down on my knees. When the prayer is complete, I hope Allah (swt) is pleased.

Draw a picture inspired by the poem above.

An Anthology of Islamic Poetry
(Excerpt of 'The Islamic Way' - Omm Khalid Samir)

LESSON 49

Copy the hadith by Prophet Muhammad (pbuh).

Prayer is the light of believers.

Colour the picture.

Nahjul Fasaha (pg 396)

LESSON 50 - IMAM MUSA AL KADHIM (AS)

Copy the sentence.

Imam Musa (as) is the seventh Imam.

Trace the sentences.

Imam Musa (as) was known as al Kadhim which means the one who swallows his anger. He was wise and generous.

Colour the picture.

LESSON 50 - IMAM MUSA AL KADHIM (AS)

Trace the hadith from Imam Musa al Kadhim (as) in any colour.

Kindness and love to people is half of wisdom.

- Imam Musa al Kadhim (as)

Trace the hadith from Imam Musa al Kadhim (as).

Your aid to the weak is of the best charities.

-- ABOUT --
Name: Imam Musa al Kadhim (as)
Title: The one who swallows his anger
Imam Number: 7
Buried in: Baghdad, Iraq

Colour the picture.

Tohfa al Uqool (Pg 425)
Tohfa al Uqool (Pg 437)

LESSON 51

Trace the Quran verse in any colour.

And Allah loves those who are pure and clean.
Quran 9:108

Copy the hadith from Imam Ali ar Rida (as).

Keep yourself clean, since cleanliness is the manner of Prophets.

Colour the picture.

Tohfa al Uqool (Pg 519)

LESSON 51

Copy the hadith by Imam Ali (as).

A believer has a cheerful face.

Trace and copy the sentence.

No one can understand your heart better than the one who created it.

Draw a self portrait

Nahjul Balagha 'Peak of Eloquence' - Imam Ali (as)

LESSON 52

Trace the sentence.

How beautiful is it that the same God who made the stars, the seas, the mountains and its peaks, the universe and its galaxies felt this world would be incomplete without you.

Draw a picture inspired by the sentence above.

LESSON 52

Copy the sentence.

Today will never come again, remember to thank God, be a good friend, encourage someone, take time to care and let your words heal and love.

Colour the picture.

LESSON 53

Trace the poem 'I am a Muslim'.

I am a Muslim, and God I praise. For all His blessings, my voice I raise. In one God I believe, no equal had He. Lord of the universe, compassionate to me. Muhammad the Prophet, taught me the way. To be honest and truthful, throughout everyday. The Holy Quran, to life is my guide. Its teachings I follow, by it I abide. Islam is my religion, preaches good deeds. Mercy and kindness, to the right path it leads. Upon all humanity, God showers His

LESSON 53

grace. Regardless of colour, nationality
or race. Through working together,
our hopes increase. To live in a
world, full of love and peace. Full of
love and peace. I am a Muslim, and
God I praise. For all His blessings,
my voice I raise.

Draw a picture inspired by the poem above.

LESSON 54 - QURAN

So seek your Lord's forgiveness and turn to Him in repentance. Verily, my Lord is Most Merciful, All Loving.

Quran 11:90

LESSON 54 - QURAN

Trace and copy the prayer.

Dear God, please keep us away from the wrong things that will take us away from you and please forgive my sins, as you are the Most Merciful and the Most Forgiving.

Copy the sentence.

Connect to God through remembrance, patience, prayer and repentance.

Draw a sunrise

LESSON 55 - IMAM ALI AR RIDA (AS)

Copy the sentence.

Imam Rida (as) is the eighth Imam.

Trace the sentences.

Imam Ali ar Rida (as) was known as the grateful one.

-- ABOUT --
Name: Imam Ali ar Rida (as)
Title: The Grateful One
Imam Number: 8
Buried in: Mashad, Iran

Colour the picture.

LESSON 55 - IMAM ALI AR RIDA (AS)

Trace the hadith from Imam Ali ar Rida (as) in any colour.

He who wishes to be the strongest of all should rely on Allah.

- Imam Ali ar Rida (as)

Copy the sentences.

I am grateful like Imam Rida (as).

I thank God for everything.

God has given me so many blessings.

Draw something you are grateful for today.

Fiqh-Ur-Reza (A.S.). P 358

LESSON 56

Trace the passage from the dua for water by Imam Sajjad (as).

O God, bless Muhammad and his household and provide us with the blessings of the heavens and the Earth. Indeed you have power over everything.

Colour the picture.

The Psalms of Islam 'Al-Sahifat Al-Sajjadiyya' - Imam Zain al Abideen (as) : Supplication 19

LESSON 56

Copy the passage from the poem 'The Kingdom of God'.

Fatima the lady of God's Paradise,
Ali the warrior, the leader, the wise.

Colour the picture.

An Anthology of Islamic Poetry
(Excerpt of 'A Kingdom of God' - Mariam Rizvi)

LESSON 57

Trace and copy the passage from the poem 'An invitation to prayer'.

Allah's love and worship had shown
me the light,
Slowly, but surely everything turned
out alright.

Colour the picture.

An Anthology of Islamic Poetry
('An Invitation to Prayer' - Tahera Rizvi)

LESSON 57

Copy the passage.

You can't break a person who gets their strength from Allah (swt). Let your faith in Allah (swt) be bigger than your fear.

Colour the picture.

LESSON 58

Trace the prayer.

Dear Lord, whatever is it I desire, may I desire you more. Whatever I seek, may I seek you more. Whatever I love, may I love you more. May you be more to me than anything in this world.

Draw a picture inspired by Ramadan.

LESSON 58

Copy the sentence.

Never go too long without watching a sunset.

Draw a sunset.

LESSON 59 - QURAN

وَمَن يُؤْمِن بِاللَّهِ يَهْدِ قَلْبَهُ

**Whoever believes in Allah,
He will guide his heart**

Quran 64:11

LESSON 59 - QURAN

Trace the hadith from Imam Ali (as).

Belief means appreciation with the heart, acknowledgement with the tongue, and action with the limbs.

Trace the passage.

Our hearts thrive in the constant rememberance of God. Remember God in all you do.

Colour the picture.

Nahjul Balagha 'Peak of Eloquence' - Imam Ali (as)

LESSON 60 - IMAM MUHAMMAD AT TAQI (AS)

Copy the sentence.

Imam Taqi (as) is the ninth Imam.

Trace the sentences.

Imam Taqi (as) was known as the pious and the generous one.

Colour the picture.

LESSON 60 - IMAM MUHAMMAD AT TAQI (AS)

Trace the passage.

We never know how our actions can inspire those around us. A small act of kindness can have a big impact on someones life. Never underestimate the power of your kindness.

Copy the sentence.

Helping others is one of the best ways to help yourself.

-- ABOUT --
Name: Imam Muhammad at Taqi (as) or Muhammad al Jawwad
Title: The Pious and the Generous
Imam Number: 9
Buried in: Baghdad, Iraq

LESSON 61

Trace the sentence.

The Quran is a powerful revelation sent from Heaven as a mercy to this Earth.

Copy the sentence.

The Quran is like a friend. The more time you spend with it, the more it will share its secrets.

Colour the picture.

LESSON 61

Trace the verse from the Quran in any colour.

We send down the Quran as a healing and mercy for the believers

- Quran 17:82

Trace the hadith from Prophet Muhammad (pbuh).

Behold! I am leaving for you two precious things. First of them is the book of Allah (swt) in which there is light and guidance... The other one is my Ahlul Bayt.

Colour the picture.

Hadith Thakalayn

LESSON 62

Trace the passage.

If you are honest, people may deceive you. Be honest anyway. If you are kind, people may accuse you of selfishness. Be kind anyway. All the good you do today will be forgotten by others tomorrow. Do good anyway. What you create, others can destroy. Create anyway. Because in the end, it is between you and God. It was never between you and anyone else anyway.

LESSON 62

Copy the prayer.

Dear Allah, please grant us the strength to do good deeds, protect us and guide us to become closer to you.

Draw a lighthouse guiding ships in the dark.

LESSON 63

Trace the sentence.

The four women of Heaven are Fatima the daughter of Prophet Muhammad (pbuh), Asiyah the wife of the Pharaoh, Khadija the wife of Prophet Muhammad (pbuh) and Mariam the mother of Prophet Isa (pbuh).

Colour the picture.

LESSON 63

Copy the sentences.

Be brave like Fatima (sa).

Be smart like Khadija (sa).

Be strong like Mariam (sa).

Be patient like Asia (sa).

Colour the picture.

LESSON 64

Trace the sentence from the dua from Imam Jafar as Sadiq (as).

O God, to Thee belongs praise for the good health of my body which lets me move about.

Copy the sentence.

The things we take for granted someone else is praying for.

Trace the words.

faith

hope

patience

reliance

gratitude

Colour the picture.

The Psalms of Islam 'Al-Sahifat Al-Sajjadiyya' -
Imam Zain al Abideen (as) : His supplication when sick

LESSON 64

Trace the passage.

You have what it takes. You are strong enough, brave enough, capable enough and worthy enough. It's time to start believing in yourself because no one else has the dreams that you have and no one else holds the same magic inside. It's time to start believing in the power of yourself.

Draw a past, present and future self portrait.

Past	Present	Future

LESSON 65 - IMAM ALI AL HADI (AS)

Copy the sentence.

Imam Ali al Hadi (as) is the tenth Imam. He was known as the guide and the pure one.

-- ABOUT --
Name: Imam Ali al Hadi (as)
Title: The Guide and The Pure One
Imam Number: 10
Buried in: Samarra, Iraq

Colour the picture.

LESSON 65 - IMAM ALI AL HADI (AS)

Trace the verse from from 'Dua Arafah' by Imam Husain (as) in any colour.

O Allah, purify us and lead us to success.
Dua Arafah

Copy the sentence.

May my heart be pure like the heart of Imam Ali al Hadi (as).

Colour the picture.

Dua Arafah - Imam Husain (as)

LESSON 66 - QURAN

LESSON 66 - QURAN

Trace the translation of Surah Al Fatiha in any colour.

In the name of Allah, the Most Compassionate, Most Merciful.

All praise belongs to Allah, Lord of all the worlds.

The Most Compassionate, The Most Merciful.

Master of the Day of Judgment.

You alone we worship and You alone we ask for help.

Guide us along the straight path.

The path of those You have blessed, not those You are displeased wth or those who are astray.

LESSON 67

Trace the hadith from Prophet Muhammad (pbuh) in any colour.

The Quran is Allah's university; so learn as much as you can in this university

- Prophet Muhammad (pbuh)

Trace the hadith from Imam Ali (as).

The Quran contains news about the past, foretellings about the future and commandments for the present.

Colour the picture.

Bihar-ul-Anwar, vol. 92, pg.19
Nahjul Balagha 'Peak of Eloquence' - Imam Ali (as)

LESSON 67

Copy the poem.

Heal your heart,
with the words of Quran.
A blessing from Allah (swt),
for all of man.

Colour the picture.

Fun Fact:
There are 114 surah in the Quran. The first is surah Al Fatiha and the last is surah Al Nas.

Fun Fact:
The Qur'an was first revealed to Prophet Muhammad (pbuh) by the Angel Gabriel in a cave on the mountain of Hira in Mecca.

LESSON 68

Copy the sentence from the book 'Be like the stars and rise'.

Prayer has many effects and blessings. Both Quranic verses and traditions talk about the impact and benefits of prayer.

Colour the picture.

Be like the Stars and Rise - Somayeh Zomorodi

LESSON 68

Trace the sentence from the book 'Be like the stars and rise'.

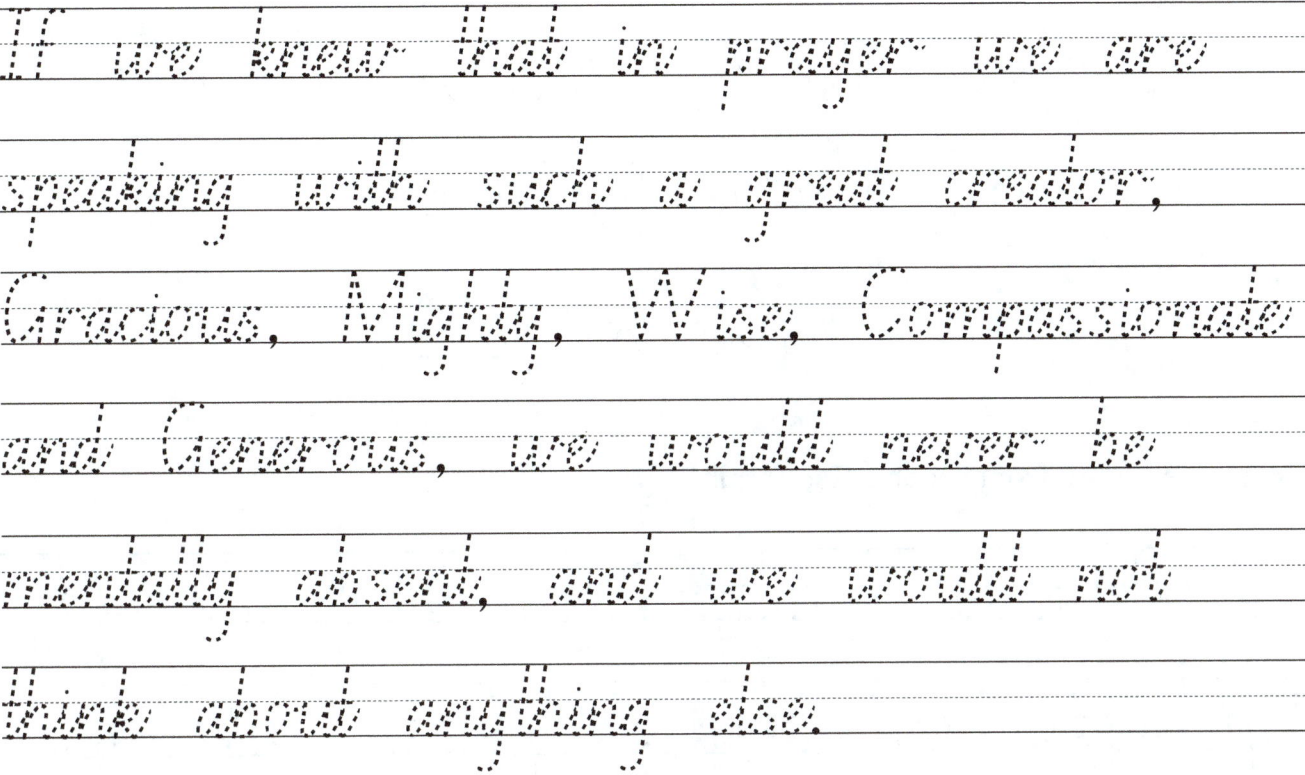

If we knew that in prayer we are speaking with such a great creator, Gracious, Mighty, Wise, Compassionate and Generous, we would never be mentally absent, and we would not think about anything else.

Colour the picture.

Be like the Stars and Rise - Somayeh Zomorodi

LESSON 69

Trace the hadith from Imam Ali (as) in any colour.

No wealth is more profitable than wisdom.
- Imam Ali (as)

Trace the hadith from Prophet Isa (pbuh).

Wisdom is developed by humility, not by pride, and likewise plants only grow in soft soil, not in stone.

Colour the picture.

Nahjul Balagha 'Peak of Eloquence' - Imam Ali (as)
Lantern of the Path - Imam Jafar as Sadiq (as)

LESSON 69

Trace the hadith from Imam Jafar as Sadiq (as) in any colour.

We encourage our children to recite Tasbihat az Zahraa as we encourage them to pray.

- Imam Jafar as Sadiq (as)

STORY OF TASBIHAT AZ ZAHRAA

The Prophet Muhammad (pbuh) taught lady Fatima (sa) a special form of remembrance that would nourish her soul and lighten the weight of her daily struggles.

The powerful practice became known as Tasbihat az Zahraa, named in honour of the lady who embraced it with devotion.

Colour the picture.

TASBIHAT AZ ZAHRAA

34 times – 'Allahu Akbar'
Allah is the greatest

33 times – 'Alhamdulillah'
All praise is due to Allah

33 times – 'Subhanallah'
Glory be to Allah

Mir'at al-Uqul fi sharh Akhbar al al-Rasul

LESSON 70 - IMAM HASAN AL ASKARI (AS)

Copy the sentence.

Imam Hasan al Askari (as) is the eleventh Imam.

Trace the sentences.

Imam Hasan al Askari (as) was known as the soldier of God.

Colour the picture.

A soldier of God is someone who is loyal to God's mission.

Everything they do is for the sake of Allah (swt).

LESSON 70 - IMAM HASAN AL ASKARI (AS)

Copy the hadith from Imam Hasan al Askari (as).

For every day has a new goodness.

Trace the prayer.

O Allah, please help me live a life were I am in service to you at every moment. Helping those who are oppressed, needy, poor, and hopeless. Please help me to apologise when I wrong others, and to always be humble, taking responsibility for my actions and mistakes.

-- ABOUT --
Name: Imam Hasan al Askari (as)
Title: The Soldier of God
Imam Number: 11
Buried in: Samarra, Iraq

Nuzhat an-Nadhir, p.50-51

LESSON 71

Trace the passage from the poem 'His Words'.

In the Name of Allah begin every action. Obey, and worship Allah with devotion. Offer salah with humility and attention. Read the Quran with understanding and comprehension. Let Allah's pleasure be our only aspiration, and success in the Hereafter, be our sole ambition.

DICTIONARY:
Devotion – Strong affection or loyalty.
Humility – The quality or state of being humble.
Comprehension – The act of understanding.
Aspiration – A goal, aim, or ambition.
Ambition – A strong desire to reach a goal.

An Anthology of Islamic Poetry ('His Words')

LESSON 71

Copy the passage from the poem 'Muhammad (pbuh)'.

Read the Quran as much as you can,
The words of Allah (swt) for the
guidance of man.

Colour the picture.

An Anthology of Islamic Poetry ('Muhamad (pbuh)')

LESSON 72

Trace the passage from the poem 'The Principals of Islam'.

Know, child, that God is only one,
And He has no partner or son; He
has made us and everything. All
beasts, all fowls, all birds that sing,
the sun, moon, the starry sky, the
land, the sea, the mountains high. He
knows whatever we think or act, by
Him is seen the real fact.

Draw three creations of Allah (swt) mentioned in the poem above.

An Anthology of Islamic Poetry
(The Principles of Islam' - Sayyed Mohammad)

LESSON 72

Trace the passage from the poem 'The Principals of Islam'.

Forever the same, no age, no youth,

He is Perfection, He is Truth.

Almighty, All-seeing, Wise, He hath

not form of shape or size. But

Self-Existing is our Lord, and is

always to be adored.

Look out your window and draw what you see.

An Anthology of Islamic Poetry
(The Principles of Islam' - Sayyed Mohammad)

LESSON 73

Trace the passage from the dua in the morning and the evening by Imam Sajjad (as).

Praise belongs to God, who created night and day through His strength, set them apart through His power, and appointed for each a determined limit and a drawn out period.

Colour the picture.

The Psalms of Islam 'Al-Sahifat Al-Sajjadiyya' -
Imam Zain al Abideen (as) : Supplication 6

LESSON 73

Trace the sentence.

When you replace "Why is this happening to me?" with "What is Allah (swt) trying to show me?", everything changes.

Copy the sentence.

May I never forget on my best day, that I still need God as desperately as I did on my worst.

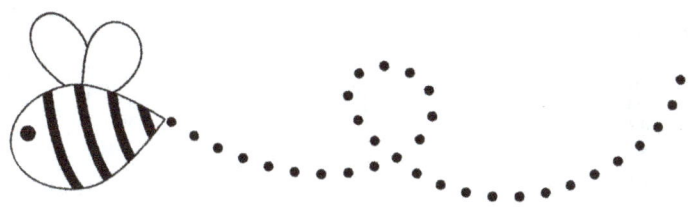

LESSON 74

Trace the passage.

Know yourself, know God and worship Him with all your heart. Let Him embrace you with His endless love and mercy.

Colour the picture.

LESSON 74

Copy the passage.

Allah (swt) created you with a divine purpose. Be the person God has created you to be.

Draw a picture inspired by the passage above.

LESSON 75 - IMAM MAHDI (AJTFS)

Copy the sentence.

Imam Muhammad al Mahdi (ajtfs) is the twelfth Imam.

Trace the sentences.

Imam Muhammad al Mahdi (ajtfs) is the last Imam. Al Mahdi means the guided one. He will fill the Earth with justice and peace.

Colour the picture.

LESSON 75 - IMAM MAHDI (AJTFS)

-- ABOUT --
Name: Imam Muhammad al Mahdi (ajtfs)
Title: The Guided
Imam Number: 12

www.ingramcontent.com/pod-product-compliance
Lightning Source LLC
Chambersburg PA
CBHW081103070526
44584CB00022B/3188